The
ART
GALLERY

STORIES

The
ART
GALLERY

STORIES

Written by

Philip Wilkinson

Series editor

Alison Cole

PETER BEDRICK BOOKS

NTC/Contemporary Publishing Group

NEW YORK

This edition published 2000 by Peter Bedrick Books
a division of NTC/Contemporary Publishing Group
4255 West Touhy Avenue, Lincolnwood (Chicago)
Illinois, 60712-1975 USA

ISBN 0-87226-634-6
First published 1997 by Macmillan Children's Books

Text copyright © Macmillan Children's Books

Typeset by Macmillan Children's Books

Printed in Singapore

ACKNOWLEDGMENTS

a = above, **b** = below, **l** = left, **r** = right

Contents page: clockwise from top left: National Gallery, London, National Gallery, London, National Gallery, London, Musées Royaux des Beaux Arts de Belgique, Brussels/Bridgeman Art Library.
Introduction: Louvre, Paris/Giraudon/Bridgeman Art Library.
8 Ancient Art and Architecture Collection/John P. Stevens, **9a** British Museum, London/Bridgeman Art Library, **9l** AKG/Erich Lessing, **9r** Scala, **10** Musée de la Tapisserie, Bayeux, with special authorisation of the city of Bayeux/Bridgeman Art Library, **11a** Arena Chapel, Padua/Scala, **11b** Arena Chapel, Padua/Bridgeman Art Library, **12** S. Maria della Grazie, Milan/Scala, **13a&b** Uffizi, Florence/Scala, **14** Gemaldegalerie, Kassel/Bridgeman Art Library, **15a** Prado, Madrid/MAS, **15b** S. Ignazio, Rome/Scala, **16** Louvre, Paris/Giraudon, **17a** National Gallery, London, **17b** Palazzo Labia, Venice/Scala, **18** Prado, Madrid/AKG/Erich Lessing, **19a** National Gallery of Scotland, Edinburgh/AKG, **19b** National Gallery of Australia, Canberra: gift of Sunday Reed, **20** National Gallery, London, **21a** Louvre, Paris/Scala, **21b** Uffizi, Florence/Scala, **21ar** Louvre, Paris/AKG/Erich Lessing, **22** National Gallery of Art, Washington: Samuel H. Kress Collection, **23b** Duomo, Orvieto/Scala, **23r** Museo Diocesano, Cortona/Scala, **24** National Gallery of Art, Washington: Andrew W. Mellon Collection, **25l** Vatican, Rome/Scala, **25r** The Royal Collection © 1997 Her Majesty Queen Elizabeth II, **26** National Gallery, London, **27a** Prado, Madrid/Index/Bridgeman Art Library, **27b** National Gallery, London, **28** Musées Royaux des Beaux Arts de Belgique, Brussels/Bridgeman Art Library, **29a** Albertina Drawings Collection, Vienna/AKG/Erich Lessing, **29b** Alte Pinakothek, Munich/AKG, **30** National Gallery, London, **31a** Private Collection/Bridgeman Art Library, **31b** Derby Museum and Art Gallery/Bridgeman Art Library, **31B** Derby Museum and Art Gallery/Bridgeman Art Library, **32** Louvre, Paris/Giraudon/Bridgeman Art Library, **33a** Uffizi, Florence/Scala, **33b** Musées Royaux des Beaux Arts de Belgique, Brussels/Giraudon, **34** National Gallery, London **35a&b** Tate Gallery, London, **36** Tate Gallery, London, **37a** Uffizi, Florence/Scala, **37b** Tate Gallery, London, **38** Museo Nacional Centro de Arte Reina Sofia, Madrid/Giraudon/Bridgeman Art Library, © Succession Picasso/DACS 1997, **39ar** Philadelphia Museum of Art: A.E. Gallatin Collection © Succession Picasso/DACS 1997, **40** Louvre, Paris/Giraudon, **41a** National Gallery, London, **41b** Tate Gallery, London © Demart Pro Arte BV/DACS 1997, **42l** National Gallery, London, **42r** Onze Lieve Vrouwkerk, Antwerp Catherdral/Bridgeman Art Library, **43l** Metropolitan Museum of Art, New York: Catharine Lorillard Wolfe Collection, Wolfe Fund, 1903, **43r** National Gallery of Canada, Ottawa: transfer from the Canadian War Memorials, 1921 (Gift of the 2nd Duke of Westminster, Eaton Hall, Cheshire, 1918), **44** © The Horniman Public Museum and Public Park Trust, **45** Victoria & Albert Museum, London, **46a** Metropolitan Museum of Art, New York; Rogers Fund, 1927, **46b** courtesy of the Rebecca Hossack Gallery, London, **47a** Victoria & Albert Museum, London, **47b** Collection Musée de l'Homme, Paris/D. Ponsard.

CONTENTS

INTRODUCTION

Since the beginning of time, people have told stories. Our earliest ancestors sat around the fire and listened to tales of heroes and heroines, gods and goddesses. Very soon, artists produced paintings and sculptures of stories. In times before most people could read or write, pictures were used to tell stories and to teach people. Medieval cathedrals, for example, were full of pictures of Bible stories that acted as visual sermons for those who could not read. Even in later times, when more people could read, artists still used story paintings to make a moral point. They used vivid effects of light, shadow and color, as well as action and gestures, to excite, delight, inform, or even terrify the viewer. Artists have continued to paint religious stories and they have recorded important historical events. They have painted myths, fantasies, stories from books, and stories from everyday life. And to each of these stories artists have brought their own individual style and interpretation.

This book explores stories in art from all over the world. It is in three main parts. First, there is a historical section which shows how fashions of storytelling have changed through the ages. Next comes a section featuring ten of the world's greatest narrative paintings, together with other works by their artists. The final section examines some of the notable themes explored in story paintings, and shows some of the variety of narrative art from different parts of the world.

THE ANCIENT WORLD

The artists of the ancient world illustrated myths and legends that had been handed down from one generation to another by word of mouth—tales of the gods, and stories about how the world was created. Another popular subject was the deeds of heroes and kings.

These images were often "stylized" (created in a particular way which does not show things as they are in real life). Important people were sometimes shown larger than the others and the episodes in a story were shown side by side, like the frames in a modern comic strip. These stylized images made the story clear and easy to grasp.

THE PALETTE OF NARMER *c. 3000 BC*

The ancient Egyptians made slate palettes for mixing colored make-up for their faces. This palette was made for King Narmer, who united the two kingdoms of Upper and Lower Egypt. The palette tells stories which show the power of the king. It was made in the traditional style of ancient Egyptian art, showing figures and beasts in profile.

This side of the palette shows one of the king's victories. Narmer is shown wearing the high crown of Upper Egypt, just as he is about to hit one of his enemies on the head. The hawk-god Horus, both a protector and a symbol of the king, holds a rope that passes through the enemy's nose.

On the back of the palette, Narmer wears the crown of Lower Egypt. In the upper section he is looking at a group of opponents who have been beheaded on the battlefield. At the bottom a bull, a symbol of the king, knocks down the walls of an enemy city.

RED-FIGURE VASE *c. 450 BC*

In Ancient Greece stories of gods and heroes were especially popular subjects for vase illustrations. This vase tells the story of Odysseus and the Sirens. The Sirens were half women, half birds and they sang with such bewitching beauty that sailors died jumping into the sea to try and reach them. Odysseus made his men put beeswax in their ears and had himself tied to his ship's mast so that he would not be able to jump overboard. As a result of this defeat, the Sirens themselves jumped into the sea and died.

These vase figures were drawn in black lines and the background to the picture was painted in with a clay solution that turned black when the pot was fired in the kiln. This left the figures standing out in the natural red color of the clay, with their details picked out delicately in black.

TRAJAN'S COLUMN *AD 113*

Roman emperors used sculptures to celebrate their achievements and to show how powerful they were. The emperor Trajan had this 98 foot column put up in Rome, carved with scenes of his victories in northern Europe. The carved reliefs run in a continuous spiral up the column.

Crossing the Danube

This scene shows how the Roman legions crossed the River Danube by tying together boats to make a bridge. The sculptor has given an idea of the size of the army by stacking the more distant figures above the men in the foreground. The soldiers' clothes and the structure of the boats have been carved in great detail.

MEDIEVAL TIMES

In medieval times, the Christian religion spread across the whole of Europe. Stories of the Bible were the most widely portrayed by artists. This was important for the church, because it gave priests a way of explaining the Bible to the majority of people who could not read. Churches and cathedrals were decorated with series of wall paintings, altar pieces, and stained-glass windows.

The artists of the Middle Ages also portrayed their own times in the lively illustrations around the edges of manuscript books and in works such as the Bayeux Tapestry.

THE BAYEUX TAPESTRY *11th century*

In 1066 Duke William of Normandy invaded England. The Bayeux Tapestry shows the events leading up to the conquest and the battle itself in a series of 60 scenes, with captions describing the action in Latin. This great tapestry is 230 feet long and 20 inches high. It was created by a team of artists on linen cloth, using several different colored wools.

This part of the tapestry shows the death of the English king, Harold, on the left. It is not certain which of the figures is the king, but the text makes it clear that "Harold Rex Interfectus Est" ("King Harold is killed"). Meanwhile, to the right, the English foot soldiers put up their last resistance.

ARENA CHAPEL, PADUA

Giotto di Bondone, c. 1267–1337

The Italian artist Giotto was most famous for his "frescoes" (wall-paintings done when the plaster is still "fresh," or wet). The huge fresco on the end wall of this chapel shows the Last Judgement, with heaven on the left and hell on the right. The frescoes around the other walls of the chapel show episodes from the life of the Virgin Mary and of Jesus Christ. By making his figures look solid and three-dimensional, Giotto was one of the first artists to break away from the flat, two-dimensional style of the early Middle Ages. The faces are carefully modeled and the shadows in the folds of the clothes are painted with great skill.

The Betrayal of Christ

This painting is one of the panels from the Arena Chapel showing one of the events leading up to Jesus' crucifixion. The Bible tells how Jesus' disciple Judas plotted with the chief priests to betray his master. Judas approached Jesus and kissed him, and this was the sign to the priests' men to capture Jesus.

Giotto has portrayed the drama of the scene by contrasting the calm stillness of Jesus' face with Judas' worried expression and heavy brow. Jesus and Judas are covered with Judas' yellow cloak. The color yellow is a symbol of cowardice and treachery. To the left, one of the disciples tries to defend Jesus by cutting off the ear of one of the captors with his sword. But Jesus told his friend, "They that take the sword shall perish with the sword."

RENAISSANCE

The fifteenth century saw a great growth of interest in the art and literature of ancient Greece and Rome. This artistic movement (called the Renaissance from the French word for "rebirth") spread throughout Italy and Northern Europe. Artists started using a technique called "perspective" which enabled them to represent three-dimensional forms on a flat surface, creating an illusion of space and distance.

Bible stories were still popular but biblical characters were painted more realistically. In addition, painters began to be interested in the stories and legends of the past, especially the myths of Greece and Rome.

St. Peter rushes forward to whisper in St. John's ear. In front of them, Judas looks up at Jesus in disbelief. Judas knows that he will be the one to betray Jesus.

THE LAST SUPPER *Leonardo da Vinci, 1452–1519*

Leonardo produced this wall-painting for the refectory (dining room) of a monastery in Milan, Italy. It shows Jesus' last meal with his disciples, a popular subject matter for a dining room. Leonardo shows Jesus' central role in the story by placing him right at the center of the picture, and by painting him slightly larger than the disciples.

This is a moment of drama because Jesus has just said to his disciples, "One of you will betray me." Leonardo contrasts Jesus' calm with the different gestures and expressions of the disciples as they seem to show their disbelief, protest their innocence, and ask who will be the betrayer.

PORTINARI ALTARPIECE
Hugo van der Goes, 15th century

This central panel from a large altarpiece by the Flemish artist Hugo van der Goes shows the shepherds visiting the baby Jesus. The artist painted the buildings as if they were in a fifteenth-century town in Northern Europe. The rich and colorful clothes worn by the angels are painted in the style of priests' clothes, contrasting with the ordinary clothes of Mary, Joseph and the shepherds, with their worn, rough faces. The large figures are particularly striking because they are painted life-size on a huge wooden panel nearly 10 feet tall.

PRIMAVERA (SPRING)
Sandro Botticelli, c. 1445–1510

The Italian artist Botticelli's painting is a celebration of the new life and loves that come with spring. The goddess of love, Venus, is shown in the center, ruling over the garden. She is accompanied by the three Graces and by her son Cupid who hovers above her head. On the left is Mercury, the god of springtime.

On the right the god of the west wind, Zephyr, pursues the nymph Chloris who, at the touch of his warm breath, is transformed into the goddess of flowers, Flora.

Botticelli shows Chloris at the moment of her transformation with flowers sprouting from her mouth. Flora is next to her so that the viewer can see the moment both before and after the transformation.

SEVENTEENTH CENTURY

The artists of the seventeenth century gave their paintings a bolder sense of drama and excitement than had been seen before. Some artists used the tricks of perspective to make subjects seem to burst out of the canvas towards the viewer, or to create the illusion that a painting was a real part of the room.

Other artists created dramas with light, illuminating the most important figure with dazzling beams shining across a dark canvas; and more unusual poses were used. All these devices were designed to involve the viewer more closely in the story the artist was telling.

JACOB BLESSING THE CHILDREN OF JOSEPH *Rembrandt, 1606–69*

This painting is based on the Bible story of Joseph. Joseph has lived in exile in Egypt for a long time, working for the pharaoh. Finally his father, Jacob, and his brothers come to Egypt. Jacob is an old man and he knows that he will soon die. Joseph brings his sons to see their grandfather, and Jacob blesses them.

Rembrandt uses a glowing light to draw our attention to the faces of the people in the painting. He portrays the tenderness of the scene, with Jacob, Joseph, and the two boys grouped closely together, while Joseph's wife, Asnath, stands to one side.

Rembrandt was fascinated by the oriental clothes of his own time and so he portrays Joseph wearing a large turban. The effect of the light on these two faces seems to bring father and son closer together.

THE SURRENDER OF BREDA
Diego Velázquez, 1599-1660

Velázquez painted this picture to celebrate a great Spanish victory over the Dutch. The Spanish artist has painted the Dutch leader bending his knee and offering the Spanish leader the key to the city of Breda. On the left is the Dutch army, wounded and in disarray. By contrast, the Spanish soldiers to the right of the painting hold up their lances proudly. Velázquez has given the background landscape a bluish tinge, suggesting its distance and making the foreground figures stand out more clearly.

MISSIONARY WORK OF THE JESUITS
Andrea Pozzo, 1642–1709

Andrea Pozzo was a member of the Jesuits, the largest Roman Catholic religious order. He painted this ceiling for the Jesuit church of St Ignazio, Rome. The ceiling is designed to tell the story of the work of the Jesuit order around the world. Pozzo has placed Jesus at the very center of the ceiling, and arranged the people from the different continents around the edge. Pozzo has painted stone arches and pillars that look as if they are actually part of the structure of the church to give the impression that the action is taking place above the viewer.

EIGHTEENTH CENTURY

During the eighteenth century many artists stopped painting religious subjects and looked for other stories. A fashion for decorative art in some parts of Europe meant that mythological and picturesque scenes were popular. As well as ancient myths, artists also illustrated the work of more recent storytellers.

Some artists also created stories from their own time. "Satire," a method of criticizing people's morals or behavior by ridiculing them, began to be popular. Satirical paintings and cartoons often did this by telling a story. Viewers were amused by these works, but they also understood the moral message.

Tiny cupids hover in the air, emphasizing that this is an island of love.

EMBARKATION FOR CYTHERA *Antoine Watteau, 1684–1721*
According to a Greek myth, the goddess of love, Aphrodite, was born when she rose out of the sea near the island of Cythera. A shrine to Aphrodite was built on the island and lovers went there to worship her. The French artist Watteau's painting is mistitled. It actually shows a group of lovers leaving the island after visiting the shrine. Watteau suggests the reluctance of the lovers to leave the island—several of them hesitate on the way to the boat, and the central woman turns her head to look back towards the shrine. The artist captures the beauty of the scene, using gentle colors and achieving the effect of a glow of warm light.

MARRIAGE A LA MODE – EARLY IN THE MORNING

William Hogarth, 1697–1764

The English artist William Hogarth painted groups of paintings that told a continuous story to make a moral point. *Marriage à la Mode (Fashionable Marriage)* is one of these groups. Its six paintings tell the story of a marriage which takes place because a bankrupt nobleman makes his son marry the daughter of a rich man. This is the second painting in the series and it is called *Early in the Morning*. Already the couple are bored with each other and with the lives of pleasure-seeking which they have been leading. On the left, a servant has tried to remind them of unpaid bills, but they have refused to pay any attention to him.

Small details suggest pastimes taken up briefly by the couple and then dropped when they became boring: a violin, playing cards, and a book on the card game whist.

MEETING OF ANTONY AND CLEOPATRA

Giambattista Tiepolo, 1696–1770

In the first century BC, the Roman soldier Mark Antony fell in love with Cleopatra, queen of Egypt, and they lived together in Egypt in great luxury. The Italian painter, Tiepolo, uses rich colors and creates an illusion of stonework to give a regal feeling to the decoration. He has dressed Queen Cleopatra in the extravagant clothes of his own time, rather than the simple dresses of real ancient Egyptian women. Antony's red cloak and the servants' turbans add to the impression of richness and luxury.

NINETEENTH AND TWENTIETH CENTURIES

At the beginning of the nineteenth century, an artistic movement called Romanticism stressed the importance of the artist's own individual feelings and ideas. This was one of many new movements to develop during the nineteenth and twentieth centuries, leading to a huge variety of artistic styles. Artists experimented with different ways of telling stories, often inventing their own individual art of storytelling.

THIRD OF MAY 1808

Francisco Goya, 1746-1828

In 1808, the French invaded Spain. Many Spanish people hated being governed by a foreign power, especially because the French soldiers were often violent. On May 2, 1808 a group of Spanish patriots took part in an uprising against the French army. The uprising failed and the leaders of the rebellion were ordered to be shot the next day.

When Goya painted the scene he did not show the faces of the French firing squad. In contrast, all the rifles point towards the central figure who is the center of attention. The anguish of his comrades is also obvious. The Spanish artist actually painted this picture six years after the event but it gives the impression that it was painted at the very moment the shooting happened.

The figure offers himself up to be shot, lifting his arms in a gesture which reminds the viewer of Christ on the cross, his white shirt blazing like a light.

THE VISION AFTER THE SERMON *Paul Gauguin, 1848–1903*
This painting shows an episode in the Bible in which Jacob wrestles with an angel, a sign of the struggles that God sometimes makes his people suffer. The French artist Gauguin painted a group of villagers on their way home from church "seeing" a vision of Jacob wrestling with the angel. The tree that stretches across the canvas separates the "real" scene from the vision. Gauguin painted the villagers in a simple, realistic style, but the wrestlers are shown in unnatural colors on a bright, red ground. The artist used this contrast to show that the struggle exists only in the imagination of the praying people.

NED KELLY *Sidney Nolan, 1917-92*
The Australian artist Sidney Nolan painted many pictures of scenes from the life of the legendary outlaw, Ned Kelly. Kelly, originally imprisoned for stealing horses when he was 12, joined a gang, robbed banks, fought the police, and took over a sheep station by force. He was eventually caught and hanged for his crimes.

Kelly had a black iron box made for himself which became his trademark. Nolan drew it using thick black paint which contrasts with the spacious landscape with its yellow ground and deep blue sky. The black box, and Nolan's pictures of it, have made Kelly into an Australian folkhero.

PAOLO UCCELLO

THE BATTLE OF SAN ROMANO

In the fifteenth century Italy was made up of many separate city-states. The Italian rulers were often at war with each other, and in 1432 the armies of Florence and Siena fought at San Romano. The Florentines won and their rulers, the Medici family, commissioned Uccello to paint three pictures of the battle. This painting shows the leader of the Florentine army, Niccolò da Tolentino, on his white horse, followed by his troops with their lances held high. Pieces of armor and broken lances lie scattered on the ground.

Uccello was fascinated by "perspective," the art of showing three dimensional space on a flat surface. He has painted the people and the horses to make them look like solid figures, and he has chosen the size and position of everything with great care. Uccello shows Niccolò's importance by placing him at the center. Many of the lines in the picture, such as the broken lances and the edges of the trees, seem to point towards his head.

Niccolò is protrayed as a brave leader. Instead of a helmet he wears an elaborate head-dress.

Uccello painted the farmers on the hill very small to show how far from the battle they are.

Uccello painted this self-portrait as an elderly man in about 1460.

Uccello's second painting shows another Florentine leader arriving with reinforcements. There are no lances or corpses on the ground, which tells us that this event took place before the battle had begun. This gave Uccello the chance to depict the more colorful aspects of the scene—the banners, rich bridles and saddles, and brightly decorated shields.

The Arrival of the Florentine Reinforcements

The third painting in Uccello's sequence shows a turning-point in the battle. The leader of the Sienese army is knocked off his horse—a moment of triumph for the Florentines. As his horse rears, a Florentine lancer pushes him backwards, and Uccello has painted him just as he is about to fall to the ground.

Bernardino della Carda Thrown off his Horse

Paolo Uccello was born in Florence in 1397. As a young man he worked for the famous sculptor Lorenzo Ghiberti and then he went to Venice, where he worked on the mosaics in the church of St. Mark.

By 1431 he was employed as a painter in Florence. His works were painted for churches and for the homes of rich Italian nobles. Uccello was a successful painter but towards the end of his life he found it difficult to work. In August 1469 he sent in a tax return to the Florentine authorities, writing, "I am old, infirm, and unemployed, and my wife is ill." Uccello lived for another six years, dying in 1475 at the age of 78.

FRA ANGELICO

ANNUNCIATION

A golden dove hovers above Mary's head. The dove is a Christian symbol of the Holy Ghost.

Fra Angelico painted his *Annunciation* in the early 1430s. The painting tells the story of the Angel Gabriel's visit to the Virgin Mary. The angel tells her that she will give birth to a son whose name will be Jesus and that Jesus will be called Son of the Highest.

Fra Angelico set his painting of the Annunciation in his own time. Mary and the angel are framed in the arches of a fifteenth-century building and Mary sits in a chair of that period. The rich colors are typical of Fra Angelico's style. Golden halos hover above the two figures and the artist has painted a cloud of gold behind the angel. The artist has placed Gabriel's hands to show the viewer that the angel is telling Mary some important news. Mary has been reading a book and leans forward to listen to the angel's words.

In the background of the Annunciation, Fra Angelico painted Adam and Eve. They are being sent away from Paradise because they disobeyed God and ate the apple from the Tree of Knowledge. This is the artist's reminder that Jesus will come to earth to save humankind from sin.

Fra Angelico included this self-portrait in a fresco for Orvieto Cathedral.

ADORATION OF THE MAGI

This large painting shows the Magi, or wise men, who came to worship Jesus, bringing gifts of gold, frankincense, and myrrh. They are kneeling before the holy family, in front of the stable where Jesus was born. The picture is filled with the Magi's servants and companions, and Fra Angelico has added some interesting extra details. The peacock on the roof of the stable is a symbol of immortality. The painting was left unfinished when Fra Angelico died and it was completed by Fra Filippo Lippi.

Fra Angelico was born in Italy between 1395 and 1400. As a young man he trained as a painter and manuscript illuminator, but in his early twenties he became a monk. He was a member of the Dominicans, an order of preaching friars. He combined the work of preacher and painter by producing many religious pictures, most of which tell stories of the life of Jesus.

When his order took over the convent of San Marco in Florence, he painted some 50 frescoes to decorate the walls. Fra Angelico became a successful and important painter. He became friends with two popes and painted many pictures for them. When he died in Rome in 1455 he was remembered as a painter "who had no equal in his art."

RAPHAEL

St. George and the Dragon

According to an ancient legend, a dragon lived in a lake close to a city. The people of the city were so terrified of the fire-breathing monster that they fed it with their sheep. When they had no more animals, they sacrificed their own people. They chose the victims by drawing lots, and eventually the king's own daughter was selected. St. George promised to kill the dragon and to save the princess and her people.

Raphael shows the scene at the moment of the dragon's death, as St. George's lance pierces its body. St. George and his white horse dominate the painting. The princess looks on, praying for her safety, that of her people, and the life of the man who is rescuing her. Raphael shows St. George as a hero, dressed in shining armor, at the moment of his triumph.

In the background, the towers of the city can be seen. According to the story all the citizens became Christians as a result of St. George's noble deed.

In his painting of St. George and the Dragon Raphael included his own name. The horse's harness is richly decorated in golden thread. Part of the decoration includes "Raphello" picked out in gold.

Raphael painted this self-portrait in about 1505–7, when he was in his early twenties.

THE SCHOOL OF ATHENS

In this large fresco in the Vatican, Rome, Raphael painted many of the philosophers of ancient Greece. The artist included Euclid, the mathematician, who is drawing a geometric shape at the bottom right, and Pythagoras, who is writing in a book at the bottom left. At the center, carrying heavy books, are Plato and Aristotle. Since no one knew what they actually looked like, Raphael gave his ancient Greeks the features of some of the artists he knew. For example, Plato's white hair and beard make him look like the great painter, Leonardo da Vinci.

Raffaello Sanzio, now known as Raphael, was born in 1483 in Urbino, Italy. His father, Giovanni Santi, was a painter, and was Raphael's first teacher. By the time he was 17, Raphael was painting in his own right, beginning to work on a series of religious paintings. In 1508 he was summoned to Rome because Pope Julius II was redecorating his apartments in the Vatican. Raphael and his assistants painted frescoes for a suite of rooms for the pope.

The fame of these paintings, with their dramatic power, brought Raphael many other commissions. These ranged from religious paintings to portraits, from tapestry designs to architectural work for the church of St. Peter's, Rome. He was busy for the rest of his short life, which ended when he was only 37.

TITIAN

BACCHUS AND ARIADNE

The ancient Roman writer Ovid told the story of how Ariadne was abandoned by her lover, the Greek hero Theseus, on the island of Naxos. As Theseus' ship sailed away Bacchus, the god of wine, caught sight of Ariadne and fell in love with her. Bacchus came down to the island on his chariot, accompanied by a band of noisy followers. He promised Ariadne a place among the gods if she would return his love. Ariadne became Bacchus' wife.

Titian shows the moment when they first met. They are visually linked by the colors of Bacchus' pink cloak and Ariadne's bright red scarf. Titian's picture was painted for the Italian prince Alfonso d'Este. It shows Bacchus stepping off his chariot, which is pulled by two cheetahs from Alfonso's private zoo. His followers run alongside, making loud music with their cymbals, tambourines, and horns. Ariadne, in a twisting pose, echoed by the folds in her clothes and the line of her scarf, is painted just as she turns to see Bacchus. The picture is brilliantly colored, using some of the most expensive and purest paints available at the time.

In the far corner Titian painted these stars to remind viewers of another part of the story of Bacchus and Ariadne. Bacchus takes Ariadne's crown and throws it into the sky, where it becomes a circle of stars.

On the horizon Titian has painted the departing ship of Theseus, Ariadne's former lover, its sails filled by the wind.

Titian painted this self-portrait as an old man, when he was the most successful artist in Europe.

Titian was born in Piere di Cadore, Italy, in around 1485. He trained in Venice with the leading Venetian painters of the time, including Giovanni Bellini. In 1516 Bellini died, leaving Titian the greatest painter in Venice. Titian's reputation spread widely. He painted works for kings, princes, and churchmen all over Europe. But Titian hardly ever left Venice, the city he loved so much.

Titian painted religious and mythological pictures and superb portraits. He worked and reworked his pictures, making them better and more detailed with each revision, until he was adding tiny touches of paint. Titian was famous for his coloring, creating marvelous effects of light, shade, texture, and atmosphere. He carried on working until he died, aged about 90.

NOLI ME TANGERE

This painting shows the appearance of Jesus to Mary Magdalene, after his resurrection. The Bible tells how Mary did not recognize him at first, thinking that he was the gardener. When she realized that he was Jesus she went forward to embrace him, but he told her quietly "Do not touch me" (in Latin, "Noli me tangere"). Jesus holds an ordinary hoe reminding us that Mary mistook him for a gardener. There is a gentleness to the way Titian has painted him, even though he is turning away from her.

PIETER BRUEGEL

THE FALL OF ICARUS

Bruegel's painting is based on the ancient Greek myth of the master craftsman Daedalus and his son, Icarus. The two men were imprisoned by Minos, the king of Crete. They escaped by making wings out of waxed feathers and flying away. But Icarus was so pleased with his ability to fly that he ignored his father's warnings about flying too near to the sun. The heat melted the wax on his wings and he fell to his death in the sea.

At first glance, this painting shows a peaceful country scene. Bruegel has painted Icarus as he disappears into the water, but the fall of Icarus only makes up a small part of his picture. None of the countrymen has noticed the tragic plunge of Icarus. They simply go on with their work as if nothing had happened.

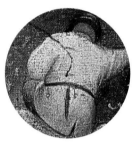

Although Breugel's painting is called The Fall of Icarus, *only Icarus' tiny legs and hand are visible as he crashes into the sea. Bruegel has hidden the story and the only clue is in this small detail. The artist is making the point that often nothing comes of people's grand ambitions.*

Even the fisherman on the bank does not look up as Icarus falls into the sea.

THE LAND OF COCKAIGNE

Old folk-tales tell of the land of Cockaigne, a place where there is a never-ending supply of food and drink. To get there, travelers have to eat their way through tons of porridge. Bruegel shows animals offering themselves ready roasted, pancakes growing on the roofs of buildings, and fences made of fat sausages. It is all too much for the three men, who have eaten to bursting-point and lie exhausted on the ground.

The picture shows that greed will bring us to a sticky end.

Bruegel made this drawing of himself in about 1565.

Pieter Bruegel the Elder was born around 1525 in Flanders. He was probably trained in the studio of Pieter Coecke, the leading Flemish artist of the time. In the 1550s he traveled around Europe, where he was particularly impressed by the scenery of the Alps. From then on, landscape became an important part of his work, forming the backdrop to large scenes of Flemish life and religious paintings.

Many of Bruegel's works have a moral point, making fun of humankind. They were often copied and printed by engravers, so that a larger audience could understand their message. Bruegel died in his forties, but two of his sons and several of his grandsons became painters.

JOSEPH WRIGHT OF DERBY

AN EXPERIMENT ON A BIRD IN THE AIR PUMP

In the glass there is a human skull submerged in milky liquid. It is a reminder from the artist that death will come to us all.

In the eighteenth century many people liked to go to lectures at which the latest scientific discoveries were explained. In a common experiment demonstrating the necessity of air for life, a pump was used to remove the air from a glass container. An animal placed in the container would collapse, and if the air was not let back into the container, it would die.

In Joseph Wright's painting, the experiment has reached its climax and the spectators are all showing different reactions. Wright has used his fascination with light to make the subject as dramatic as possible. The faces of the lecturer and spectators, the bird, and the air pump itself are brightly lit so that they stand out of the gloomy background. The wild hair and staring eyes of the lecturer add a touch of theater. This dramatic painting is full of tension. Will the lecturer let the air back in and allow the bird to live?

The elder girl hides her face because she cannot bear to look at the experiment, while the two lovers are not watching because they are only interested in each other.

Joseph Wright painted this self-portrait when he was about 40.

MIRAVAN BREAKING OPEN THE TOMB OF HIS ANCESTOR

An old Persian story tells of Miravan, a young man who saw an inscription on the tomb of one of his ancestors, promising that there was untold treasure inside. When his servants opened the tomb all they found was a skeleton and another inscription saying that the "treasure" is simply eternal rest and peace in death, something which Miravan has disturbed because of his greed. Wright's painting shows the moment when Miravan realizes his mistake and turns away, full of remorse for what he has done. As in most of Wright's paintings, lighting makes the subject still more dramatic. A lamp hanging from the ceiling illuminates Miravan, his companions, and the skeleton in the tomb.

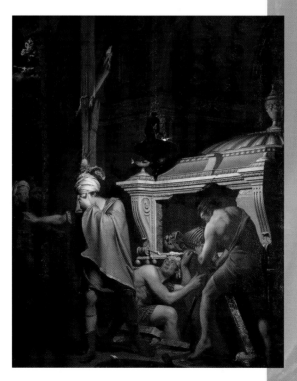

Joseph Wright was born in Derby, England, in 1734. He studied with the portrait painter Thomas Hudson and set up as a portrait painter in his home town in 1757. He was soon also producing landscapes and narrative paintings, often depicting his subjects at night, with dramatic lighting effects. Wright visited Italy in the 1770s, where he was impressed by moonlit landscapes, firework displays in Rome, and the aftermath of the eruption of the volcano Vesuvius, all of which he painted on his return to England.

Wright was fascinated by new scientific discoveries. Like his other favorite subjects, they gave him the chance to paint unusual lighting effects. He continued to paint in this way until 1797, when he died at home in Derby.

JACQUES-LOUIS DAVID

THE OATH OF THE HORATII

The outstretched arms of the three brothers draw the viewer's eyes to the shining swords at the center of the painting. The swords show clearly that there is a deadly fight to come.

David painted this picture in eighteenth-century France but the event he shows took place in ancient Rome. A Roman historian tells how a war between Rome and its rival city was decided by a fight between three warriors from either side —the Horatii brothers and the Curiatii brothers. Sabina, a sister of the Curiatii, was married to one of the Horatii, while Camilla, a member of the Horatii family, was betrothed to one of the Curiatii.

David shows the moment at which the three Horatii brothers swear to their father to fight for the honor of Rome, their city. The brothers stand close together, with their arms around each other, to show that they are united. They raise their arms towards their swords to indicate that they are swearing their oath. Their stiff poses, flexed muscles, and shining helmets show that they are ready for the fight. David's message is that duty and patriotic loyalty are important.

Two women sit slumped in grief, while another comforts her children. They cannot bear to look at their men-folk or the swords, because they know that whoever wins, one or more of their loved ones may die. Only the young boy looks up at his father, suggesting that one day he too will be a soldier.

This self-portrait was painted in 1790–1, when David was 43.

THE DEATH OF MARAT

Jean Paul Marat was a leader of the French Revolution. He was murdered in 1793 by a woman called Charlotte Corday, a member of a rival party. Marat was working in his bath, something he often did because he had a bad skin disease which was soothed by the water. Corday stabbed him with a bread knife. David's portrait shows Marat just after the murder, with the letter from Corday asking to see him still in his hand. David painted Marat as a younger, more handsome man than he was when he died, in a much more heroic pose.

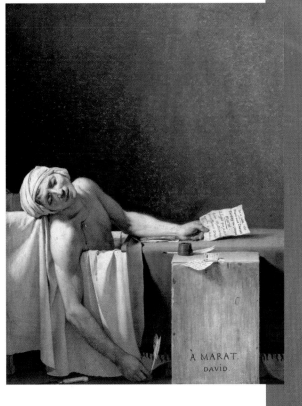

Jacques–Louis David was born in 1748. He trained in France and later studied in Rome. He began to paint in the neo-classical style, copying the art of the ancient world and painting subjects from the mythology of Greece and Rome.

David took part in the French Revolution, painting portraits of the revolutionary leaders. He was a supporter of the leader of the revolution, Robespierre. When Robespierre fell from power, David was imprisoned and narrowly escaped execution. After his release he became a friend and supporter of the new leader, the Emperor Napoleon, painting pictures to glorify the emperor's reign. When Napoleon fell from power David had to move to Brussels, where he died in 1825.

TURNER

THE FIGHTING TEMERAIRE

Turner used a very small brush called a rigger which is specially designed for painting ships' rigging.

All his life, Turner was fascinated by ships and the sea and by the luminous effects of light. In 1838 he saw an old battleship being towed by a steam tug so that it could be taken to be broken up. It was the Fighting Temeraire. Turner immediately started to make sketches of the ship on some little cards he had in his pocket. When he painted the scene, he brought out the contrast between the Temeraire, bathed in the gold and silver light of the sunset, and the black tug. Turner saw the difference between the two ships as the contrast between two ages: the old age of sail and the coming age of steamships. The blazing sunset seems to emphasize the fact that it was the end of an era: never again would elegant sailing ships like the Temeraire sail the seas.

Turner used his favorite colors of pinks, yellows, reds and whites to create the impression of a blazing sunset.

Turner painted his self-portrait in around 1798, when he was in his early twenties.

SNOW STORM: HANNIBAL AND HIS ARMY CROSSING THE ALPS

Hannibal was a general from ancient Carthage, North Africa, who marched his army across the Alps on elephants to attack the city of Rome. Turner painted the soldiers sheltering behind rocks. He shows them lit by the sun, just visible through the clouds as the violent storm rages above. The huge swirls of dark clouds and snow suck the viewer into their midst. The force of the storm and the frightened soldiers emphasize the fact that the soldiers were terrified of crossing the mountains, and many of them died because of the appalling weather.

Joseph Mallord William Turner was born in 1775 in London, England. He went to the Royal Academy Schools in 1789 and later traveled all over Europe painting landscapes, seascapes, and subjects from history and mythology.

To begin with, Turner's landscapes were painted in a very realistic style, but later he developed a dramatic and dazzlingly original style that was more suited to conjuring up atmosphere and the drama of nature than depicting details. As a result, Turner's paintings became less popular and when he died his studio was full of unsold works. He left 300 oil paintings and around 20,000 watercolors and drawings to the British nation.

MILLAIS
OPHELIA

In Shakespeare's play Hamlet, Ophelia is at first loved by Hamlet, but he later rejects her. Hamlet kills Ophelia's father and this, together with Hamlet's rejection, drives her to madness. Ophelia finally commits suicide, drowning herself in a river.

John Everett Millais was a member of a group of English painters called the Pre-Raphaelite Brotherhood. They aimed to paint from nature, using the bright colors of real life. They also liked to choose subjects from literature. Ophelia gave Millais a literary subject with the chance to paint a beautiful natural scene. Millais found his background on a riverbank in Surrey. He painted the riverside plants with minute accuracy, including details mentioned in Shakespeare's play, such as the willow tree that overhangs the water. This took him nearly four months. Then he painted the figure of Ophelia herself in his studio. His model posed in a bath of water which was kept warm by lamps underneath.

Millais included many symbols in his painting of Ophelia. The poppies are symbols of death and daisies represent her innocence.

The willow tree is entwined with nettles, representing pain and betrayal in love.

Millais painted this self-portrait in 1880, by which time he was a successful artist aged 51.

THE BOYHOOD OF RALEIGH

Sometimes Millais invented his own stories. This painting shows an imagined episode from the life of the famous English sailor and explorer Walter Raleigh in the sixteenth century. The young Raleigh and his friend, who have perhaps been playing with the toy ship in the foreground, look fascinated as a sailor tells them about life at sea. To show that the sailor has obviously been on a long voyage himself, Millais has painted two birds that have been brought to England from overseas behind him, next to the anchor. The sailor points out to sea, hinting at the lands Raleigh himself will later explore.

John Everett Millais was born in 1829. When he was young he showed artistic ability and went to the Royal Academy Schools in London at the age of 11, the youngest ever pupil. In 1848 he and a group of other artists founded the Pre-Raphaelite Brotherhood. At first Millais and the other Pre-Raphaelites were criticized but, with the support of important art critics, their work soon became popular.

As Millais became increasingly successful, his time was taken up with painting portraits of famous people and illustrating books by British writers of the time. In 1896 he was elected President of the Royal Academy, the highest honor for a British artist. He died the following year and was buried in St. Paul's Cathedral.

PICASSO

GUERNICA

During the late 1930s, a bitter civil war raged between the Nationalist and Republican parties in Spain. On Monday April 26, 1937, German bombers, flying for the Nationalists, bombed the small town of Guernica, in northern Spain. The bombing was heavy and relentless, and fighter aircraft machine-gunned civilians who tried to hide in the fields. Many innocent people were killed.

In early 1937 Picasso was commissioned by the Republican Spanish government to produce a mural for the coming World's Fair in Paris. The bombing of Guernica inspired Picasso who painted this picture as a memorial to the people of Guernica and as an expression of his anger and sadness at the horrors and brutality of war. This huge and powerful mural, about 26 feet wide, is an image of grief. The trailing arms and legs of the woman in the foreground, the cries of the figures on the left and right, the distorted faces of the bull and horse—all these elements express the grief of the survivors, and the revulsion of the artist himself.

The woman on the left of the picture cradles her child in her arms. The infant's head and arms hang down, showing that the child is dead.

The horse's hip has been pierced by a lance and it is crying out in agony.

The sheet of white light represents the explosions of the bombs.

Simple triangular shapes suggest the flames of the fire caused by the bombing.

Picasso painted this self-portrait in 1906 when he was 25.

Pablo Picasso was born in Malaga, Spain, in 1881. For much of his life he lived in Paris, where he was at the center of developments in modern art. He worked in many different and original styles, each of which he pursued with immense creative energy.

At many times in his career Picasso painted scenes of human suffering. During the Spanish Civil War, Picasso, like most artists and writers, supported the Republican side. He painted several pictures of subjects connected with the war. After the Civil War, Picasso continued to work in many different media. The sheer amount of work he created up to his death in 1973, together with his own endless inventiveness, has made him the most famous artist of the twentieth century

VERSIONS OF A STORY: NARCISSUS

The story of Narcissus was a tale told by the Roman poet Ovid in his book *Metamorphoses*. This title means "transformations," and the book is full of myths which involve one person or thing changing into another. Narcissus was a beautiful young man who fell in love with his own beauty. He turned away from anyone who loved him, including the nymph Echo. All he could do was stare at his reflection in the water, until he eventually pined away and died. He was finally turned into the flower we know as the narcissus and Echo vanished, with only her voice remaining. The story of Narcissus has been a popular subject with artists who have each treated it in their own individual way.

ECHO AND NARCISSUS
Nicolas Poussin, 1594–1665
The French artist Poussin tells the final part of Ovid's story in his gentle, expressive style. Narcissus is lying by the pool, but he is already weak. The artist has painted Narcissus as a Roman youth of real physical beauty, but the plants by his head remind the viewer that he will soon turn into a flower. Echo is portrayed with softer, gentle brushwork as she looks on sadly. Cupid, the young Roman god of love, stands nearby but he cannot help Narcissus who has turned away from love.

Poussin painted Echo as if she is fading away. This is a reminder that only her voice is left at the end of the story.

NARCISSUS

Follower of Leonardo da Vinci, 16th century

This Italian artist concentrated on the face of Narcissus himself. Narcissus is portrayed as a youth dressed in sixteenth-century costume. The artist has given the youth a wreath of leaves, something which usually suggests that someone is a poet. The youth is staring into a large bowl of water, as if he is fascinated by what he sees, and the lake in the background is another reminder of the story of Narcissus.

Dali also shows us Narcissus admiring his own beauty, at a time before he fell in love with his own reflection.

THE METAMORPHOSIS OF NARCISSUS

Salvador Dali, 1904–1989

Dali painted the story of Narcissus in the dreamlike, distorted style used by the Surrealist painters. Surrealist painters often portrayed objects which the viewer would not expect to see together in reality or which were in the process of changing into something else, making it an ideal style for the story of Narcissus. Dali has painted the large figure of Narcissus on the left, sitting by the edge of the pool, and his head already seems to be changing. To the right, an enormous stone hand holding an egg mirrors the shape of Narcissus. A narcissus flower is emerging from the stone egg, as if from Narcissus himself.

The god of snow is experiencing his own transformation as he starts to melt. This is a sign that winter is over and that spring, the season of Narcissus and his flower, is on the way.

STORYTELLING DEVICES

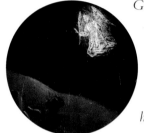

Artists use many different devices and techniques to help the viewer see who are the most important people in a painting, and to make what is happening in the picture clearer. Putting the most important person at the center, lighting particular areas, arranging the scene so that something or someone points towards the main character, are all ways of making the meaning more obvious.

THE NATIVITY AT NIGHT
Geertgen tot Sint Jans, c.1460-1490
This painting of Jesus' birth shows how an artist can use light to emphasize the important parts of a picture. The bright light from the figure of the baby Jesus illuminates the faces of the Virgin Mary and the angels and highlights the miraculous nature of the story.

Geertgen shows two scenes simultaneously. In the distance another miraculous light appears, as an angel comes to tell the shepherds on the hillside about Jesus' birth.

THE ABDUCTION OF REBECCA
Eugène Delacroix, 1798–1863
Delacroix's painting shows a scene from Sir Walter Scott's novel *Ivanhoe*. The French artist painted the moment when Rebecca is kidnapped by the wicked knight, Bois-Gilbert. The knight's servants are forcing her onto a horse and Bois-Gilbert looks on impatiently, ready to ride away, while the castle burns in the background. Delacroix captures the drama and excitement of the scene. The brilliant colors bring the painting to life. Everything combines to suggest rapid movement and powerful action: the prancing horses, the twisted bodies, the flowing clothes. The effect of movement is strengthened by the artist's loose, flowing brush strokes.

THE DEATH OF GENERAL WOLFE
Benjamin West, 1738–1820

General James Wolfe was a British general who won a famous victory against the French in Quebec. Wolfe himself was killed in the fighting and the American artist wanted to portray the general as a hero who laid down his life for his cause. So he deliberately based his painting on Rubens' *Deposition* (left). Like Jesus, Wolfe is surrounded by grieving friends as his body slips to the ground. The tall shape of the flag is designed to remind the viewer of Jesus' cross.

DEPOSITION *Peter Paul Rubens, 1577–1640*
The deposition, or the removal, of Jesus Christ's body from the cross gave artists a chance to portray Jesus himself and to show the emotions of his followers. Rubens used dramatic lighting to highlight the most important areas of the painting—the body of Jesus and the faces of those around him.

Rubens painted Jesus' body so that it makes a strong, single, downward-pointing line from his left hand to his feet, adding to the dramatic impact of the painting.

*A strong diagonal line leads from the top of the flag, through Wolfe's body, to the ground.
As in the* Deposition *the central figure is brightly lit and blood drips from his side.*

STORIES AROUND THE WORLD

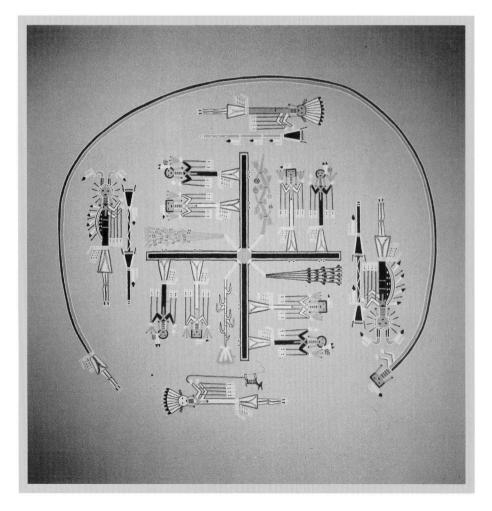

All over the world stories have been used as subjects for works of art. Artists have used their skills to portray stories from the lives of their gods or to explain ideas about how the world began. They have told traditional tales and recorded famous historical events. Different cultures have developed their own individual styles of visual storytelling using a huge variety of artists' materials, providing a fascinating record of the world's stories.

NAVAJO SAND PAINTING
20th century

For the Navajo people of south-western USA it is important to maintain a good relationship with the world of the spirits. One way of doing this is to perform a special ceremony which includes the creation of a sand painting. Sand, charcoal, pollen, and cornmeal are all used to produce the different colors in the painting, which is usually erased after the ceremony.

This painting shows the Navajo story of the creation of the world. According to tradition, four previous worlds have existed before; these are represented by the four pairs of figures in the center of the painting. The delicate lines were produced by pouring minute amounts of different colored sands onto the ground.

FOLDING SCREEN   *17th–18th century*

This Japanese folding screen is painted with the famous story of two rival generals during the clan wars of the twelfth century. The figure crossing the river is Kjikawa Kagesue. He beat the other general across the river by using a trick, telling his rival that his saddle girth had come undone so that he would stop and check.

As in many Japanese paintings, the main subject takes up only a small part of the scene. Japanese artists often show their figures against a landscape and make them stand out clearly against a plain background. In this picture the artist covered the whole screen with gold leaf and painted over it. The strong contrast between the black and the gold is very dramatic.

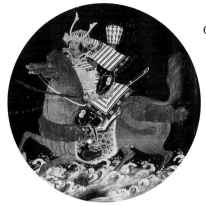

General Kagesue stands out clearly against the black background while the other general has been painted onto the gold leaf. Kagesue is pleased that his trick has worked and is smiling, but his rival has been painted with a frown. Both generals are wearing the traditional armor of overlapping layers of steel, iron, and leather.

KRISHNA OVERCOMING THE NAGA DEMON, KALIYA *18th century*

Krishna is one of the many Hindu gods. He is a popular subject for Indian artists. This painting shows Krishna's fight with a "naga" ("serpent") demon called Kaliya. Kaliya was one of the creatures who hid in the sea during the daytime and came out at night to attack wise men who lived peacefully by the coast. The tremendous strength of this picture comes from the use of swirling curves and powerful straight lines. The artist has painted the waves of the sea using fine curved lines. The body of the serpent is drawn with bolder swirls but Krishna himself stands out against the curves, as he stands upright and determined to beat the demon.

The firm straight lines of Krishna's arms and body show his power in overcoming the waves and the demon.

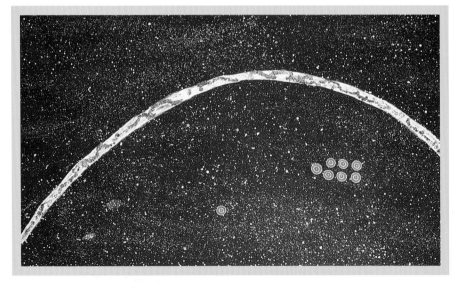

MILKY WAY JUKURRPA

Norah Napaljarri Nelson, 1991

Norah Nelson is an Aboriginal artist, well-known for her Milky Way paintings. This picture tells the story of seven Jukurrpa women who are being chased by a Jakamarra man. The women, in a last attempt to escape, turn into fire and rise into the heavens to become stars. The artist uses a special technique in which paint is lightly flicked onto the surface, producing the effect of a galaxy of stars.

WEDDING HANGING *19th century*

In China it was the custom to put up an embroidered hanging around the bed when a couple got married. The figures portrayed were embroidered in the traditional style which often had particular meanings for Chinese people at the time. This wedding hanging was designed to show that the main aim of marriage was to produce children. It shows an imaginary scene in which the children play happily. The dragons are a traditional Chinese symbol of good fortune and new life. The boy on the far left is carrying a "scepter" (special rod) with tassels which means that everything will go as the couple wishes.

This boy is holding up a type of mouth organ called a "sheng." The Chinese word for "to be born" sounds the same as "sheng." The inclusion of the mouth organ means that the couple will have many children.

PALACE DOOR *19th century*

This door comes from a West African royal palace and the carvings attached to it have a symbolic meaning. At the top a chameleon (lizard) has been placed between the moon and sun. This tells part of the story of creation. According to a West African legend, God created the earth and then sent the chameleon out to inspect it. The chameleon walked around slowly before returning to tell God that the earth was not yet dry enough. On the lower panel of the door there is a snake swallowing its tail. This is an African symbol of eternity.

INDEX